An old story retold
by Friedel Steinmann (drawings)
and Dieter Kohl (text)

WILLIAM B. EERDMANS PUBLISHING COMPANY
GRAND RAPIDS, MICHIGAN

The story told in
this book is very old.
For thousands of years
it has been written down
and passed on. And for
good reasons. For in
it we see something
of the character of man
and the nature of God.
And neither of these
has changed to this very day.

Many years ago there lived in a small village in the mountains of Israel . . .

Sea

Phoenicia

Sea of Chinn

Mediterranean

Israel

Jordan

Joppa

. . . a man who had been given the name Jonah by his father.

Like all the other villagers, he went to work every day . . .

. . . was content with himself and the world . . .

Ah! . . . parsley soup!

. . . went to church like all the rest . . .

It's gonna be a hot day today, huh, Jonah?

DING-DONG

6

10

Soon they came to an agreement. The following morning the ship left the harbor with Jonah aboard.

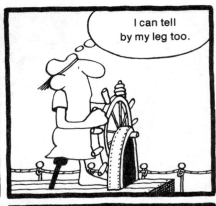

14

But nothing helped. Sooner or later the ship would sink. A great fear came over all of them, and everyone prayed to his god.

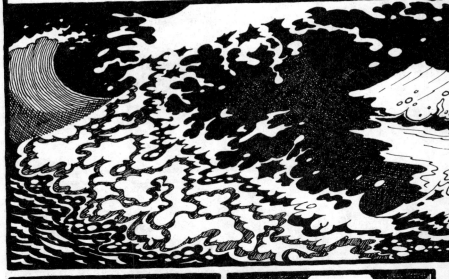

All this went unnoticed by Jonah. He lay fast asleep way down below deck.

18

22

And the storm died down at once.

27

Meanwhile God sent a big fish, which swallowed Jonah up . . .

And God answered his prayer.
The fish spit Jonah out again.

JONAH!

Go to Nineveh and preach there what I tell you.

This time Jonah went.

Jonah entered the city.

Gate's clear again!

Citeee maps!!

You got some a little easier to handle?

Nineveh was a really big city.

Boy, oh boy . . .

35

He walked around for a whole day.

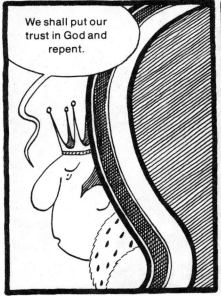

45

When God saw
how they turned
to Him again, He
repented
of the evil
He had said
He would do, and
He did it not.

48

That night . . .

52

56

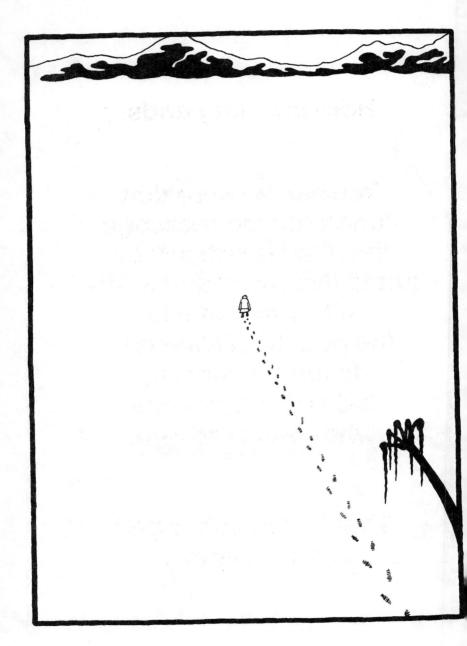

Here the story ends.

**You can be sure that
Jonah got the message
that God is concerned
about this world and is infi-
nitely merciful to
the people of Nineveh,
to Jonah himself,
indeed to everyone
who returns to Him.**

**That has not changed
to this very day.**